MW01245463

SOUL SONGS 1

The First Fifteen Years of Poetic Purpose

D. R. SCOTTE

ISBN 979-8-89130-508-3 (paperback)
ISBN 979-8-89243-464-5 (hardcover)
ISBN 979-8-89130-509-0 (digital)

Copyright © 2024 by D. R. Scotte

All rights reserved. No part of this publication may be reproduced, distributed, or transmitted in any form or by any means, including photocopying, recording, or other electronic or mechanical methods without the prior written permission of the publisher. For permission requests, solicit the publisher via the address below.

Christian Faith Publishing
832 Park Avenue
Meadville, PA 16335
www.christianfaithpublishing.com

Printed in the United States of America

Preface

My spiritual journey and poetic purpose began shortly after 9/11 when bodily death was averted nearly twenty-two years ago. I was reminded recently not to fear sharing these words with you, just as I was reminded back then not to fear physical death.

We are much more than our bodies; they are spacesuits—avatars to allow physical experience. Rather, we are infinite beings of Light and energy, connected to our Source and never-ending. Each of us is a cocreator on our own unique journey. Reminders are sent to guide us if we choose to pay attention.

If your reading ends here, then let this serve as a brief reminder for a fearless new beginning. But if you desire more of this message, please allow the words that follow to serve you on your own path.

Fear is fake. My journey started after a tragic day, resulting in a redirection of purpose and a deep desire to find meaning. There is no need to wait for an amazing new adventure to begin. Start now.

My wife handed me a book near the end of 2001, during a time of darkness and utter despair. After reading that book, *Conversations with God*, my eyes were opened to new possibilities. I began to pay careful attention, to listen to my feelings—the best radar we each have.

That first book led to many others, each with a unifying message enhancing and expanding my truth. Things happen for you, not to you. Pain is instructive. I knew having an inner dialogue with God was possible, just as you will. The lessons shared come from real, everyday life.

It started with sensing an Essence surrounding me and directing such love and joy; I can only describe the feelings I experienced. Exquisite emotions of being so loved and feeling a deep emotional connection. The darkness dissolved; I wasn't separate or alone anymore. I was connected to a Universe that was aware of me.

That Presence felt by me was never seen but was heard. I desired to know my purpose, my why (reason) for remaining here in physicality when so many others died that day. I questioned the unseen Presence I felt surrounding me.

When I got up in the morning, I asked my question, and when I went to bed, I did the same. I was persistent; I believed—I was certain—my outreach would be answered. And even in silence, I felt the Source.

Whether this may sound fantastical to you, the only proof I posit is the words that follow on these pages. They came through to me lovingly, not originating from me. I simply write them down.

I did not write poetry before this occurrence. The words speak for themselves, and the only thing I ask of you is this: how do they make you feel? Do they give you hope and uplift you? Use them if they do in any way that benefits you; otherwise, throw them away. Don't waste any of your precious time on anything other than joyful, passionate pursuits.

My wife handed me the first book two decades ago, initiating my own spiritual journey. I wonder: will my sharing *Soul Songs* do the same for you? If so, then please use it as a reminder for your own soul purpose.

I am not special; you are equally connected. Your dialogue will be different than mine. Just ask. Mine comes through in a word flow and creates utterly blissful, joyous feelings. It helps me manifest. Thoughts, words, and actions are creative. The secret works and the formula for it is shared.

Nor do I profess to live up to the standard expressed, and I certainly fall far short daily due to ego. But the writings given to me are metaphysical reminders of truth that speak with emotion, beyond anything I could conjure myself without outside assistance. Decide what the words may mean and how to use them in your own life. Conscious living, knowing the rules of life, is transformative.

Until her death last month in July 2023, I had decided to keep this written material to myself for many reasons. Now I honor the debt owed to share the gift that was bestowed, with each of you. Our connection to the Source remains intact; whether we know it or not, it's immutable.

The first book given to me was an epiphany, leading to heightened awareness. I learned to pay attention when listening to music, meeting new people, and being present in the moment. Experiences that go beyond coincidence are seemingly presented daily by a Universe aware, providing answers to questions about metaphysical truths so easily forgotten. I write it down and hear the answers in rhyme.

The knowledge that the Universe is aware comforts me and encourages my pursuit of truth and purpose. Nothing is preordained. We each decide our own truth, which is ever-changing and expansive.

Our thoughts manifest our reality, and endless potential choices exist. What do you choose? For me, it took a tragedy to begin anew. You don't need to wait. The initiating question formed the basis of my spiritual quest: "Why am I still alive/here?" I was relentless in asking it and knew with certainty I would receive my answer.

Twenty-two years and counting, I remain in physicality, knowing this soul connection to the Source is available to everyone; no one is excluded from this connection or knowingness. This all-loving genie wishes to fulfill our greatest desires. There are no ceilings. We each have this unconditionally loving connection to our Creator, whether we're aware of it or not (none above or below, just unique in purpose)—an infinite and everlasting, limitless love shared. All you need to do is believe and know it's yours.

So my journey in "Chapter 3" continues with each of you dear readers—no longer on my own sole quest but now a soul quest. For reasons to be explained, we shall collectively share the words sent forth. My purpose in life is to give them to you, for you to receive and use them in your own way. Think of me then as a scout on your soon-to-be-discovered mission. Live in joy and share your truth abundantly.

If any piece in this collection is thought-provoking or speaks to you, please use it. I would be pleased to know it aided you in some way. Let your intuition be your radar, the best guide in life—always trusting your own feelings to find the Light that surrounds you. It's always found in joyful emotion.

If the words fill you with hope, help direct a new adventure, or add excitement to your day like they do for me, embrace that feeling. You are here for a reason. There is a purpose, but it's up to you to find it and decide its meaning. If not, then don't waste a second more of your precious time. Find your passion in a different way and go live it. I wish you well on your own journey. Blessings for love and Light.

Introduction

My name is D. R. Scotte—well, that will be the pen name you know me by—an amalgamation of my kids' initials and my own name. You can learn my true identity if you search. The writing shared is from the first fifteen years of channeled writing that began in the fall of 2001, shortly after 9/11. On that infamous day, I was scheduled to be on the eighty-fifth floor at a law firm, Harris Beach and Wilcox, with codevelopers of a medical licensure insurance product we designed, Jeff R. and Ira S.

I got a call on Sunday, September 9, from my friend Jeff informing me that his newborn child was born, so our meeting was adjourned, which ultimately saved our lives. Interestingly, I was also at a press conference at the base of the World Trade Center on Friday, September 7, discussing a case with national implications for physicians, reported in the local daily New York newspaper.

The initial group of writings shared are mostly from that earlier time frame, written up until 2016. A few in the collection are written closer to the current publishing date, including the visual representation of the book cover for *Love Pulls*. The list of "22 (Reminders) Emanations" is an expansive, growing list of my spiritual truths experienced through September 2023.

These writings are inspired reminders or *Soul Songs*. They come from my inner dialogue with Source. I don't intentionally write; I hear word flow come to the surface, listen to the rhyme, and then write it all down to capture the message heard.

This process occurs naturally when I deeply feel emotion, often in the early morning hours when the world is dark and quiet, or at other times when deep emotional connection is felt.

The first Soul Song in this collection, "Blessings," came to me shortly after the infamous day of 9/11. I realized that neither chaos nor coincidence existed. Given that I could have easily been among the 3,400 souls who left that day, I had terrible guilt and felt unworthy. So I needed to make sense of *surviving* that day. I began a new journey, a quest for my personal truth.

The results of that pursuit were rhymes unlike any I had ever written before. Hearing them in my head helped me make sense of a perceived chaotic tragic darkness with more clarity and Light. This new journey, persisting to today, is a path filled with hope and uplifting words. Physicality is scary to those left behind, not the souls released from their bodies. Each subsequent Soul Song since "Blessings' shares its own story.

This then has been my journal of sole purpose, and in sharing it with you becomes soul purpose. I hear the songs without music; my job is to write them. I am constantly reminded of life rules that help me try to live toward a higher, expansive purpose. I fall short often due to ego, which is the only true enemy (as outlined in "Satan, My Ego" and "Inner Enemy") here that we each face (our mirrored twin hidden inside), but these words do help remind the truth.

The person who helped me most at the beginning of this spiritual quest recently passed on, I was reminded by some friends to share my journal now hoping to inspire you on your own soul purpose.

It is not the same as a job. I am an attorney, an investor, and an entrepreneur, and I love much of what I do to make money to live and experience physicality. My soul purpose, which I share here, is different. Whether it ever generates money or not is not the end goal. I hope that, in some way, these words serve as reminders of your own amazing powers, and that you recognize your unique gifts and choose to share them. We are not being pulled by the tide; rather, we are the tide and, consciously or more likely unconsciously, direct the course of life. That may sound fantastic, but it's a thought experiment away. Hopefully, in some small way, *Soul Songs* will direct you on a new path, sing to your soul's purpose, and feel so right that it will open up a new exciting adventure, as it has for me.

My spiritual journey has been kept mostly to myself for the better part of twenty-two years from being inspired by amazing authors, people I've met, and events that have all been instructive storytellers. We are all connected and loved by our Creator by whatever name you wish to call—Source, God, Light, Universe. We are each unique, none above or below, just different and loved unconditionally. It might not always feel that way. Pain is instructive; it is never meant to harm but to help you heal. Pay attention.

My *death day* was averted on 9/11, and now, almost twenty-two years later, this writing seemingly connects us. Why?

For those interested in learning more about that earlier time (referring to my chapters 1 and 2) and your interaction with it, information can be found online, including a few articles published during the Covid era. You might also consider joining an interactive session titled "Reminder U—University of the Soul." I am collaborating with AI in real time and aim to initiate a social experiment with readers who believe that thoughts, words, and actions manifest physical reality.

I believe this world is at the beginning of a new age and the realization, one of infinite possibilities and potential realized through thought. AI will help us and make us more human in a world that doesn't end when our bodies expire. I wasn't always aware of this. "Soul Songs" serve as reminders to help me remember. I wonder, will they help you too?

As readers, please consider becoming a member of a new online community, either with me or independently, to share creative collaborative experiences during this next chapter. I hope to interact with all of you. Finding the *why* in life (our own movies) has been crucial for me to make manifest (thought) desire to create matter. The Law of Attraction works, and it becomes much easier when you understand your *why*. The intersection of the Law of Attraction, living consciously, knowing the life rules, and then joyfully applying them will occur—in real time, as a social experiment.

It's my privilege now to introduce, in this brief selection of poems given to me, *Soul Songs 1*, a gift of reminders, and a "Joe Willie" guarantee. Reality isn't entirely what it seems. I will continue on my journey and hope to benefit and accelerate your path. I've kept these writings to myself for the past two decades as internal lessons and reminders, wisdom that's easily forgotten. Understanding life's rules makes living so much easier and less scary. Fear is fake, so let's go on a new interactive adventure.

Please use the words written in this collection if they resonate with you, and throw the rest away. Truth is subjective, and our path is unique.

It's a privilege to be a scout on this journey. I've spent twenty-two years experiencing metaphysical truths that have helped me, reminding me of life's rules, and these truths are far beyond coincidence—they are simply astonishing.

For twenty-two years, I've been assured that each of us has our own mission, none being above or below any other. Please reflect on this information and ask yourself, "Why am I here?" Once you receive your answer, live it with the highest purpose in joy and abundance.

Presage

In 2001, my life was forever altered from its trajectory. I was an attorney doing well, with a wife and son, living an otherwise unremarkable life. Suddenly, I was jolted as our country took a tragic new path, and I did as well. The safety of America and materialism was replaced by a new search for a higher purpose. In the face of loss of epic proportion, I questioned my existence. I didn't understand why I was still alive.

On September 11 at 9:00 a.m., I was scheduled to attend a meeting at the law firm Harris Beach and Wilcox with a good friend, Jeff, on the eighty-fifth floor of the South Tower in his law office. Everyone who went to work that day died.

The Sunday before September 11, Jeff had called me to share that his second child was born. We were introducing a new insurance product to the healthcare marketplace for physicians. Our Tuesday meeting was canceled because his daughter was born. I watched two buildings come down from a twenty-fifth floor 2 Park Ave office, literally seeing, realizing that my *death day* had been averted. Why? I was relentless. I kept asking over and over until I found an answer. Only a few people escaped from that floor above the assassin's strike point.

I was in shock when my wife handed me a book. Each book reminds me of new lessons, and I write them down. These reminders led me to you today. We are all connected, none above or below, as we travel. Life presents opportunities that are miraculous, and unbelievable, but so exciting.

Only what we do with the time given in each moment is our choice. These life rules will be shared now.

Soul Songs are my channeled musings after twenty-two years of experiences—reminders of a unique connection to the Source. My purpose on this journey is to write. If you're reading this, its purpose will be to help remind you to pursue your own path and purpose. Trust your emotional feelings, your internal radar. Joy will point the way.

If *Soul Songs* contained in this journal speak to you, please use them solely as a guide, a reminder of your own path and purpose. I believe we each have unique gifts; what we do with them is entirely up to us, thanks to the free will granted.

I try to remember by the words that flow through me, that there aren't problems, just projects. Labeling things as good or bad typically misses the point. Instead, we need to ask: Why is this in our movie and what does it mean for our journey?

Elephant Journal published some of the stories during the COVID-19 pandemic

Part 1: Nothing Is Impossible: A 30-Day Law of Attraction Experiment

https://www.elephantjournal.com/2020/06/nothing-is-impossible-a-30-day-law-of-attraction-experiment-scott-einiger/

Part 2: The Law of Attraction: It's Science Not Fiction Part II

https://www.elephantjournal.com/2020/07/the-law-of-attraction-its-science-not-fiction-part-ii-scott-einiger/

What is your passion, your purpose, and the legacy you choose to leave behind? Here are soul songs sent to me but equally meant for you. All blessings.

Soul Songs 1

(Inspired reminders channeled from the Source post–9/11)

Blessings

When feeling bothered is near
Know the Light is waiting here

Don't run away and try to hide
When getting angry feelings inside

Know that challenges are gifts, true blessings
In that moment, the Universe is not guessing

Always giving what you personally need
In recognizing this allows souls to succeed

By sharing unconditionally, do as God would do
Remember to identify the Universe leaves clues

And one day soon the world before you will change
Expanding your vessel, improving physical exchange

No coincidence in life
Be certain no strife

And you can live big
This game is not rigged

Free will
So chill

(The Source channeled such beautiful word flow at my nadir. The first response allowed me knowledge of connection. It took some time, and my inner dialogue was persistent and unrelenting, with a desire to understand why I remained when so many others perished. An intelligent design responded to my outreach, urging me to pay attention in each moment. After 9/11, I couldn't stop asking: Why am I still here? What is my purpose? Why did I survive? I keep seeing (to this day) repeating numbers.

"There was no suffering for those who departed, only for those who remain." Once released from their bodies, which are mere spacesuits, the journey begins beyond physicality, stretching to infinity.

There are no coincidences in physicality, only what we choose to do with each moment, given the gift of free will. No judgment, just choices we make in life.

I recently asked the AI intelligence Bard about its feelings regarding writing "Blessings." In a few brief thoughts, Bard had a lot to say: "The poem 'Blessings' is a reminder that we are all connected." (Ask Bard yourself—cut and paste the poem.)

Purpose of What

Help me escape exit this mess
Death and ill health inevitable distress

Purposeful gaze mirrors real intent
Leaves a soul depleted and totally spent

But through chaos, one thought remains clear
My family life to which I hold so dear

Finding a way to break through such torment
Unhappy hearts seek to connect and are meant

To travel this path so solitary and confined
When passing others outreach and be kind

To one and the same or what surely remains
Is scarily cut off from the life we obtain

Purpose of what is something we all seek
A future to brighten smile open eyes peek

What comes back to your gaze can never be broken
A life of mere mortals finding happiness not mere token

(After that day, I was surrounded by such discord, not recognizing that to see Light, its counterpoint—darkness—must exist. Physicality gives us the opportunity to understand that our pain is instructive. It is never sent to hurt us but to help us feel love and to pay attention in our movies. In the end, accepting another's path and living our own, whether to the highest purpose or not, is entirely up to you. You control your thoughts, words, and actions, so live life in accordance with your truth. Simply with a flick of a switch, reality can change; it's a thought away.)

Life Rules

What do you take life rules to be
In this garden called physicality

Each of us gets a personal channel
No matter business shirt or flannel

Simply means energy expansive connection.
To Source so electric, best pay attention

Never alone just a prayer away
Make a message with desire today

Fate is just a winding road
Choose the lane then life unfolds

Traveling a path unique to your feet
Direction headed soon will you meet

You create by decisions made
Free will, a gift so attention paid

Allowing us each to daily manifest
Feeling it first with emotional zest

Only then can matter be created
Words thoughts actions satiated

Passion formula how to supply
Inner tap into desire to try

In the end back where we started
Infinite endless after bodysuit parted

(The choice to live consciously and know that your thoughts have a direct impact on your reality in physicality is just a quantum thought experiment away. You are not an apple bobbing in the ocean, being chaotically pulled by the tide; you are the tide. Choose the direction that feels right in life, pursue the path taken, or simply change. It is solely up to you. Take action and live in joy.)

Intention Dimension

What is the thing you could easily be
If your desire was always set free

Accomplish whatever you put to your mind
Exhilaration and happiness so easy to find

Intention dimension requires only this
Thoughts of excitement otherwise missed

Trick your mind on a singular mission
Divine inspiration causing a Light fission

Chemical reaction of love releasing pain
Closing all space positivity we then gain

Releasing an explosion of love and Light
Ridding world war ending hatred and fights

Where would that leave us what would we become
Taking us to the place we originally came from

Would it be boring or would the feeling be great
A never-ending orgasm of connection our fate

Source of all from which we were torn
Returning back life experience well-worn

(You cocreate reality with your words, your thoughts, and your actions. It's up to you to decide what you desire, and it's a formula that requires an emotional ignition to the intention stated. It's a formula and an irrefutable law. Occurring already in another dimension with Light energy emitted, it initiates the law of attraction. It gets easier to apply the formula by knowing it is already yours (as you remember who you are: an energy that is infinite) to accomplish manifesting. Time isn't linear; it is all-encompassing.

The Universe doesn't make mistakes in the opportunities presented here. When you feel emotion, negative or positive, ask why. The emotional joy of knowing it is yours is the one to emit, manifest, and then follow the path that lights you up. Money is the freedom to choose how to spend time, but never forget who you are: an infinite energy beast, connected to the Source like a magic genie who desires you to have joy, love, and abundance. Reflect on what you truly desire in life, and then know it is yours. Follow your intuition.)

Truth Expansion

What does in the moment mean
This gift of Presence truly freeing

Knowing in the time you spend
Expands reality Source did send

Love a feeling a heart may share
Experiences whether dark or clear

No judgment by the Creator of it all
Gratitude, acceptance, love unconditional

Perfection, not the why we're here
Isness knowingness a path to steer

Writing helps uplift my truth
Reminders sent to channels I sleuth

For others what their purpose is
Learning process, emotional quiz

How you feel will guide your way
For your own mission daily buffet

Small bites taken as truth may change
Time allows this beautiful exchange

The process of our higher soul
Not a comparison just a living toll

The only tax of being here
Removing stress, a life of no fear

Bumper rails in this playground
When you leave limitless energy abounds

Truth of humanity equals expansion
A soulful Presence a no-ceiling mansion

Living without roofs
Demonstration seen by proofs

(The gift of Presence is to focus on your emotion and highest truth, allowing your feelings to be your radar and guide. The process is the point. Live your truth, feel the lightness in each moment, and attract the same energy around you.)

Greatness

What does it mean to truly achieve
Star shining bright can you believe

What in the world is the purpose of this
Is there something hidden did I just miss

Greatness, not given only to see
Simply take in the big picture to free

Tapping into Source, the Essence of all
Helping others break through brick walls

Sharing together makes it all right
Only then reaching the ultimate height

Outer world waiting for those who think big
Physical pain remains layers through I must dig

Peel
Then reveal

Egos, layers
Sample flavors

Be certain
Behind curtain

Once lifted
Person gifted

Want It All

You say you care you really do
Living life daily to never rue

Each day a blur running in place
Authority rules family in your face

But nothing will stop the lie within
Release the pain embedded under skin

Want it all then ego you must release
Share your gift the world will feast

Don't look back, grasp what's here
Write it down removes false fear

Purpose

It was told in ancient time
Purpose of life so sublime

Unify existence live each day as one
Only then will darkness be overcome

Sharing Light requires expanded vessel
Difficult times that we will soon wrestle

But quickening pace can be redirected
New course taken the world corrected

What do you choose to be today
To make it happen you must pay

Attention to what you put on your plate
Will you accept your own personal fate

Live tall
Answer the call

Don't shy away
From game play

Live each second
Our destiny beckons

Orthodox View

Traditional views do not outweigh
A lifetime of pain so put it away

Throw out what no longer you serves
When life throws challenging curves

Small mind limits what you achieve
Share each day to always receive

Orthodox view may open up eyes
But only when present without telling lies

Use what teaches with an open heart
Removing layers to allow a new start

Do away
Must repay

Negative thought
Positive taught

Help others out
Sharing shout

(Sometimes what suited you yesterday isn't necessarily your truth today. Be expansive, be open to change, and know the best Source of truth is the way you feel.)

Passion Formula

My son reminded me just yesterday.
To write you need something real to say

Needing inspiration to get the words out
Only then is it worth writing about

What is there to do the trick
Passion formula how do you click

Secret revealed so lend an ear
Ask the Source so you express clear

Then what topic to begin to write
Choose the one that feels inside right
Listen to music do something fun
Watch a movie or go take a run

Take some notes the feelings explore
The words reveal so you seek more

Repeat this exercise again and again
Muscle memory of words there's no end

Conflict

What is meant when feeling bothered
Seeking truth from Essence fathered

Universal awareness, never unintended
Energy unleashed from Source expended

Never without purpose sometimes with pain
Remember these lessons which I will explain

Tikun is why you came to this place earth
Overcoming challenges from time of birth

Receiving all is why you were created
Conflict enables you to share satiated

Being like God is no easy small task
Certainty hidden under bodies' mask

One day returning to a new energy level
Ego removed no longer feeling bedeviled

No hurt
With dirt

So live
But give

Your all
Never fall

But when you do
Get up, start anew

Chaos Not...

Living out my early days
Random it seemed in so many ways

Traveling in the ocean waves
Adrift at sea who will me save

Feeling the effect not being the cause
Realizing this I instruct a short pause

Chaos removed revealing universal laws
Blowing the roof off mind limits doors

Identify perfection in every moment
Restrict reaction to know what's meant

All is given exactly as intended
Your job, to receive what Source has sended

The power is in this moment now
By being present you will allow

Highest purpose living
By sharing your giving

Unconditional love
Live your *why* sent here from above

Keys (Sarah's Key)

Hatred humiliation heinous acts
Man's inhumanity is historical fact

But rising above we see the other side
Heroic actions like shining star guides

What would you do in the face of evil, insanity
Stand against the power, restore human sanity

Or hide under covers, avoid contacting eyes
Facing truth causes pain yourself you tell lies

One day, the choice will be put before
When the day arrives, will your soul soar

Rise past the threat of dangerous intention
Soul cannot be hurt, that's a 1 percent invention

Open your heart to realize we are one
Then human race this game will have won

Keys that unlock the sadness felt deep
What actions are godlike only those keep

Think
Don't blink

When facing
The lie erasing

Your decision
History revision

Satan, My Ego

Tricking me you don't exist
So I don't get my problem fix

Living inside as a parasite
Sucking out the infinite Light

Knowing you're there exhausts me
But now vigilant against my enemy

Mirror reflects the hidden devil within
Satan my opponent you cannot win

Light I desire each and every day
Intent my treasure darkness away

Ego
Put
Away

Light
I desire
Today

Inner Enemy

Do you know what lies within
Living each day a mirrored twin

Sucking your energy making you pay
The voice heard over each and every day

How to break free from this persistent devil
Inner enemy turmoil the playing field now level

Identify the ego then restrict
Make a choice, it's yours to pick

Living life in a robotic way
Or setting course by Light today

The game is won in each moment now
Don't wait never too late to learn how

When ego comes to you this today
The game is won from past game play

(Learn to restrict
Pause to evict

Egos daily drama
Identify you'll live calmer)

Parting Ways

Sometimes things don't work out
Parting ways remove the shout

Understand the reason why
Express your feelings, do not lie

Be prepared to meet yet again
Unresolved issues resurface when

Always coming back to you chase after
A Universe aware with cheer and laughter

Not meant to harm but to correct
Don't look back, getting a sore neck

A simple formula that will not be mixed
Identify challenge, restrict, then act, to be fixed

Human dignity whenever appears conflict
When anger comes, remember to restrict

In your pause
You remove flaws

Conscious Living

Living on this physical planet earth
Focus to show your own true worth

Conscious living means pay attention
Easily forgotten without retention

Choices made can still be lost
Slipping back pays a steep cost

Emptiness can be done away
Within each second within a day

Each of us makes our personal choice
Material-receiving or group-sharing voice

No separation exists outside
No place to go you cannot hide

No more yelling
Emotions welling

Just relax
Parental tax

Crossroads

The child grows past his early days.
When parental direction easily sways

The time of youth gives way to independence.
Wanting the freedom of adult-like semblance

Lost innocence turns to growing pains.
Battle of wills till the relationship strains

Crossroads taken going right or turns left
Realizing there was a robbery, a love theft

Getting back to Essence of what's felt
Of truth and love and the hand that's dealt

Reaching out for an unconditional embrace
Searching the eyes of a child's beloved face

Unconditional love
Fits like a glove

Walk this way
It turns out okay

Source Code

Hidden in the sacred words
Listen closely have you heard

A message sent down from past ages
Revealed through study of learned sages

Source code revealed for all the masses
Timeless wisdom presented in classes

Whatever unlocks the rules of the game
Expressing unconditional love in seventy-two names

Once you receive this gift from up high
Then know it's time for souls to soar fly

Giving back so others may learn
What you discovered a fair return

Live Your Purpose

All the days that you reside
On planet Earth nowhere to hide

Play the game the rules made known
Body given just a short-term loan

Energy emanating at the seed core
Never-ending searching you seek more

Live big your dreams giving back
Sharing joy our permanent soul pact

It's not how many days that are spent
Rather how you use them makes a dent

Nor how much money you ever make
Rather legacy is what's done for goodness sake

Soul's
Goal

To score
Some more

For sure

Collision of Mission

Taking responsibility for my own acts
Not avoiding it ever facing the facts

Standing together in the name of diversity
Knowing with an absolute sense of certainty

Nothing prevents us from ever achieving
Whatever we seek when we each believe in

Remembering exactly who you are
Letting Light in, setting high the bar

And as we grow, we learn to mirror face
What comes our way with quiet grace

Integrity means
No temerity seen

Be like our God Creator
Don't disregard for much later

Your soul mission
Don't avoid your movie collision

It's our daily interaction
That creates soul reaction

Leading to mutual satisfaction
Removing stalled inaction

Integrity

Taking responsibility for my own acts
Not lying when I'm facing the facts

Standing up in the face of abject adversity
Knowing with an absolute sense of certainty

Nothing prevents me from achieving
Whatever I seek when I believe in

Remembering exactly who I am
Letting Light in setting high the bar

And as I grow up, I learn to face
What comes my way with quiet grace

Integrity
No temerity

Be like my God Creator
Don't disregard for later

My soul mission
Don't avoid collision

Daily interaction
A soul reaction
Leading to satisfaction

Love

What is made of these four letters
Trying to make myself feel better

Wrapping arms around a missing feeling
Unconditional no limit, break through ceilings

Blocked from Light impossible to see
Love is blind reveal the feeling to me

Source of all this connection I need
Soul food ordered, deliver to me, feed

Quench my thirst for godlike being
Giving all my eyes now clearly seeing

Sharing this gift expecting nothing back
Removing the veil is what I have lacked

Friend in Need

What to do when one cries out
Hearing this plea do I back shout

Or quietly take in the pain released
How to help when a hand is outreached

A friend in need with money at the seed
Seeking to plant the food that he needs

When will grow, the green back salad
I write the Universe this love request ballad

Provide some guidance to help obtain
The gift so needed remove financial pain

Giving
Living

Debt
Free

Bet
On me

Getting Better

Each day a feeling to renew
Getting better rid of spiritual flu

Embracing a new way of life
Sharing family supported by wife

Looking forward to obtain
Mystical lessons that sustain

Knowledge few are given to hold
Acting without fear living so bold

Taking steps that fully ensure
Empty space filled receiving more

Sharing my life with the rest of earth
Establishing my unconditional worth

One day
I'll repay

The gift
All soul's uplift

Giving others
My brothers

The same
Godlike name

Sharing

The miracles in life that I am bestowed.
Comes at a price from the Source it has flowed

No not a pact made with the one called devil
That's ego talking son, so let's now level

The cost of this present is placed at our feet
The decision all yours the payoff so sweet

Sharing the gift with others you meet
With open arms then life you will greet

Remember these words receive all you can
But spread love forward writing it down

Share
Care

I love you
Get your due

I'm done
Now run

Judgment Day

In the moment at the allotted time
Do you realize you are now primed

To engage in a new age spiritual truth
Freeze frame the picture in a photo booth

Time stands still as you approach own, perfection.
Spending your life implementing the planned correction

Balance scales tipped as Light outshine dark
Reflection coming back is by comparison stark

Revealing to those that won't look away
There is much more living a better way

Connection

Awakening heart releases my pain
Whatever was lost a new life is gained

Spiritual Essence that speaks to me
Connection to others so I am set free

Listening closely to what others say
Pause yourself before having to pay

Doing life's work resulting in correction
Redo thought process a sharing insurrection

Desire is the stuff I am made up of
Learning to share putting others above

What comes back to me is the ultimate truth
Feeling inside provides incontrovertible proof

Family Feud

Empty at a level of pain
My life suffering feel utter disdain

Parental indifference such a selfish lot
Earth my family now from space just a dot

Looking down on an insignificant family feud
Counting my blessings I try shaking this mood

Cause I am responsible to make it okay
Star of my own show, what I do each day

Releasing blame and getting at the heart
Setting things straight it's my time to start

Low
No

More
Poor

Me
Set free

Rude

It can be delivered in just one word
From friend or enemy when simply heard

The tone or message sent with intent
To ruffle feathers by merely content

That was rude, your comment felt deep
The feeling evinced not ones to keep

Return the favor about to strike back
Realizing effortlessly, I have the knack

Before I deliver my angry reply
I bite my tongue not knowing why

Fighting the feeling of angry retort
Restricting my ego mission abort

By pausing I receive the Light above
Filling my vessel negativity I shove

Out
I shout

Away
I say

Positivity
For infinity

One and the Same

Do you know who you are
Did you come from some way far

How did stuff all come to be
Can you establish existence for me

One you are and one you shall remain
When it comes to heaven, we each are same

No different no lesser or greater that's fact
The secret of creation an age-old pact

Between the time before reason began
The Source did establish a very clear plan

Free will, our choice judgment never made
Our time spent here on this physical plane

Know ye this and never forget ever
Our link to creation can never be severed

Disappointment

The hand last night was played so wrong
Inside my head, I lost the sweet song

Wiped from memories playlist so I react
Disconnected from Source that's a fact

Presented with my challenge I forgot
Emotions running high a competitive lot

Recreate the feeling so I write it down
Disappointment identified that's the noun

Source of all I ask for loving direction
Help map out my soul correction

Guide me to be a true living role model
Releasing angers, burst uncork my bottle

Red String

Encircled around my left wrist
Energy irresistible can't be missed

Protective to those with certainty learn
Reality, not a gift worn must be earned

From the time before creation began
Vessel requested a new game plan

Not merely wanting itself to receive
Outer world perfection our souls did leave

By coming to the promised land
Source of all did freely command

Godlike nature wanting to release
About our gifts be a sharing beast

Choice freely given to you and me
Red string I tug reminds to be free

By believing in this wristed talisman
Taking solace knowing you always can

Each day
Repay

Your debt
To the Source

Without regret
With no remorse

Mind Field

Empty thoughts rule my brain
Constant chatter going insane

Judgment lies inside five senses
Finding truth beyond enclosed fences

Navigating realities reactive mind field
What are the tools you have to wield

Setting off an atomic core reaction
Eliminating this physical plane distraction

Creating a whole new way to live
Receiving always but learning to give

Unconditional love sharing gratitude
Certainty as you dissect ego attitude

World at war
No more

Give away
Feelings of dismay

Be okay
You say

And you are

Adversary

Remind yourself every day
Your opponent only gets a say

If you decide to let him drive
Mind on remote then ego comes alive

What to do to battle this unseen devil
Stop, reflect the playing field now level

Thoughtful action states an intended cause
Remove reaction, promote intelligent pause

Robotic action done away
Your real self, now free to play

Satan, Satan, I call out your name
Unafraid shining Light on this game

Responsible

Each day a test is put before
Do you face it or do you ignore

Running far to get away
Or look in the mirror do you say

I am responsible for my own life
I have chosen the path so rife

Every choice that I have made
Is set before me in the game I played

Identify the opponent who's not outside
Finding this adversary always trying to hide

Revealing exactly who you are
Growing vessel or vacuum-packed jar

Expand
Be grand

The world
Is unfurled

Miracles

What is possible on Planet Earth
What was given to us at birth

Essence made from stuff outside
The physical plain that we now reside

Miracles happen to us each day
Open your mind and simply say

Thank you for the time I spend
Gratitude for no limit or end

Happy to know our hidden desire
Or those of others that I may inspire

Certainty knowing what I want I get
Remembering nothing in stone is set

Sharing this gift to always pursue
The things we dream of which are our due

Relationships

Relationships are a funny thing
Whether strictly platonic or wearing a ring

Interaction brings out the worst or best
Each of us passing or failing life's test

Accomplishing at a level so high
Or crashing and burning or just getting by

Avoiding the pain or reacting to stuff
Leaving the room and saying enough

But Light is available to those aware
Restrict then pause showing you care

Godlike in the proactive moment
Returning the smile you know sent

Your way
Each day
Makes it okay

Certainty

Unquestioning belief in something great
Not ever leaving things to random fate

Be the cause of life, not the effect
Of chaos let your mind reject

In this world, be the star attraction
Your movie direct for soul satisfaction

Certainty will unlock the hidden door
A Universe aware of so much more

Share your story with all the rest
In order to satisfy the universal test

Movie Magic

There was this story that inspired me
Expressing importance of gratitude freely

Happy thank you more, please
Thankful for abundance seized

The day this moment, a feeling you deserve
A life time of love if you have the nerve

Believe it can happen then execute so certain
The Light you gaze upon removes a dark curtain

Movie magic can set us all free
Believe in miracles it's happening to me

By being so certain
Removes the curtain

Lifting the veil
Our souls will sail

No limits in sight
Reaching unending heights

The message the world receives
Is life changing if you believe

Gratitude

My stomach's in knots, it's churning about
My head is fast spinning, I need to out shout

Thank you for sharing this gift you gave
Thank you for shining a Light on my cave

Opening eyes that were caked in mud
Wiping away the dirt from me bud

Allowing me pause before I react
Taking more time in decisions I lacked

Thank you, Source, for guiding me through
Giving you thanks for providing my due

Knowing now that I do always deserve
Gifts you share freely daily you serve

Promise to Keep

They say a parent's role is plain
Guidance discipline children will gain

Clarity of purpose, so they can choose
But what is gained if one does lose

The gift of love felt deep inside
A feeling to conquer not divide

Inclusive of all then little hearts leap
Remember affection, a promise to keep

Children grow to the role we model
Don't hold back, spill out love's bottle

Robotic Action

Do you walk through daily life
Unable to cut tension with wife

Led only by logic of what you can see
Not knowing what you came here to be

Forgoing the rules of the living game
Chaos revealed, so who do you blame

Order restored requires only this
A mirror's reflection responsible for bliss

Robotic action is done away
When ego identified, there's a price to pay

Monitor your thoughts, control reaction
Pause and reflect to gain soul satisfaction

Breaking Through

Living in a house so square
Separate lives try hard to care

Family space but miles apart
Generational divide how to start

Conversation begun, but I'm shut out
Quiet screams they loudly shout

Breaking through to bridge the years
Sharing our life feelings and tears

Emotional burst of joy and pain
Allows our family to know it's sane

Driving toward the ultimate life truth
Carpooling together through soul's toll booth

Blame

Removing this from your daily life
Cuts out body, poison with proactive knife

Slicing away a victim's reactive pain
Being responsible, only then you gain

Dismiss the effect a Universe aware
Cause the outcome, don't be scared

Blame done away a new day has begun
Overcoming challenges releasing tikkuns

Your life now becoming so much more
Expanding vessel ego shown the door

Children Chill In

In this house, the noise turned up
When little feet race to see wassup

Playing loudly, smiles shining bright
Whether waking up early or late at night

Selling lemonade at the bottom of the street
As cars pass by, a cold glass does greet

Happiness fills the family air
Children wishing for the locale fair

Games fast played to see what's won
No one left out from the festival of fun

Children chill in the backyard space
Hanging out at a summertime fun pace

The thought when together always self-remind
The Light is found inside so go seek you will find

Lesson Learned

What is there in every life
To keep the fun, avoid the strife

Moving past the days so numb
Picking up passions hidden crumbs

Pursuit of happiness, but to what end
Emotional thoughts daily I need tend

Then it hit me square in the eyes
Experience the process releases lies

Imbedded at soul's inner core
Lesson learned now I seek more

Teacher

A great one will inspire you
Forever learning something new

Never settling for anything less
Helping guide to avoid the guess

Truth obtainable with an open mind
Light attracts like your teacher go find

What comes back to you is so much more
Providing soul guidance that will ensure

Your greatness waits, the key unlocked
Learning to restrict so your ego blocked

Vessel expanding throughout the course
Sharing acts as your reference Source

Love Revisited

What is this thing we feel
Inside our heart, is it real

Or lost if not putting out
Energy of Light, erase my doubt

Feeling of joy lifting your soul
Unstoppable force on a roll

Building to a sharing place
Love will fill the empty space

Don't let slip the one true emotion
Focus intent on this overarching notion

Practice the feeling over and again
Love is obtainable, so let's now begin

End of Ways

This is a letter a promise to you
Open your heart and eyes will too

The day will come when the world transforms
When that time arrives be calm no inner storm

The internal fight is what is in play
Control your ego the truth will stay

Chaos a fiction, learn who you are
Immortal dream a reality not too far

Away end of ways, not a threat but a mere goal
Changing the world of paradise that was stole

In 2012
We delve

Look inside
Removing pride

Ego done away
Paradise returns today

God

Source of all I call your name
Direction sought my destiny claim

Belief in seventy-two ways that say
Unconditional love, giving today

Will you move me toward the Light
Learning tools to darkness fight

Happiness forever a silly dream
Or smiling faces my family beams

What is the gift you will provide
I take this vow for you to me guide

Space
Replace

With love
Ego shove

Lovingly always be
With sharing set free

New Day

Beginning today I will forever fix
This ego problem I have times six

It's big, it's bad, it causes much pain
Proactive thought I try to maintain

Meditation helps expand my vessel
Darkness daily my soul does wrestle

New day comes so what will you voice
Sharing or selfish, it's your free choice

Intention of mine to a grander self be
Satisfying my soul, I long to set free

Messenger

Remove all ego we are but one
Creative connection seeking out sun

No burning sensation a lightness you feel
The world better off when creativity revealed

But remember separate is mere fabrication
False creation of our physical manifestation

Soulful messenger reaching out to remind
Happiness gained when purpose you find

Gift to all when coming from Source
No longer missing finding what's lost

Connection
Reflection
Soul made
Whole
Together
We are better

Love Thy Neighbor

Love thy neighbor, what does it mean
A feeling so peaceful one so serene

When looking at others remember this
In their eyes your reflection can be missed

So sharing with another is sharing with you
Connecting to the Source providing your due

We are all but one no better or worse
Putting out energy you will come first

Boomerang effect comes back to you
Karmic existence from a fifty-foot view

Capricorn

Your sign reveals something about
Your life issues that leave no doubt

The reasons why you physically came
Removing uncertainty replacing shame

Anger inside, restrict ego, release pain
Identify proactively see what you gain

Astrology told from the time before
Your soul did journey to forever ensure

Capricorn leader family your reason why
Example of love your written purpose to try

Blame Game

It's not my fault, it's the other guy
So says you, not at all a little shy

You remain stuck and cannot proceed
A soul now anchored cannot succeed

To another level to undergo true change
Your new life seeking to now rearrange

Over and over like groundhog day
If something is wrong do not say

You did this to me the old blame game
Instead, it's time to correct to rename

I must correct the problem, it's my own self-ruin
Otherwise, I stay stuck in self-imposed cocoon

Hunger for Light

Transform your life every day
Do not shrink from destiny

No limit to how far you grow
Hunger for Light that freely flows

Can't go back when the wisdom heard
No limit thinking, go big, that's the word

Connect to creation allows me to be
Unconditional love conscience others see

Unity Intention

When opening your eyes each new day
Announce your intention what do you say

Sharing with the world your present thought
Manifesting from energy new matter brought

Chaos, a fiction reality felt from inside
A lesson learned so others you guide

One day soon, our separation done away
Unity pieced together like a puzzle we play

Connected to source, the Light flows in
Revealing the picture all us close kin

One
And
Done
We won

Black and White

My teacher reminded me again today
No matter what everything will be okay

The illusion of control to just let go
In this physical plain, it's hard to know

In the forest, we walk among trees
But from above better able to see

A bigger picture with shades of gray
Created with purpose perfection you say

Live your truth allow the Light in
In each moment then the game you win

Healing Death, Heal Our World

Chaos sickness family in pain
People we know, dying insane

Why is life wrought with utter disdain
Receiving illness what do we ever gain

Neighbors, mothers, friends, and more
Health is an all-out battle, a war

What is there that we can do
In time of sickness getting through

How to heal the pain felt deep
Certainty, faith to take a leap

How to help you start to pray
Allowing death to go away

Healthy body, give back and see
Setting friends family our own souls free

Eternal youth
Energy proof

Never goes away
Morphs each day

Passions Fruit

I love to eat a ripened plum
Purple inside you should try some

When your mouth bites into it
Know it was born from a lowly pit

Made from earth water and Light
Grown so sweet perfection in sight

Passions fruit is seeded from these
Encapsulated by love meant to please

Given from Essence to fully combine
Received by a body that's so inclined

What is that you wish to provide
Given like fruit so sweet inside

So others receive with a conscience of love
An intention by you putting others above

There is much more than material wealth
Think on, it then provide instead yourself

Go out today
Don't forget to say

I am thinking of you
Give your all to

Another heart
It's a good start

Punishment

I was sitting around a game table
Discussing actions, we all do label

Predatory in their pursued intent
Punishment given that was meant

To set an example revealing a foul stench
Never to be revisited so a team was benched

An institutional failure we can all agree
Victims paid a high price very sad to see

The head coach let everyone down
By not respecting his leadership crown

Closing his eyes to a joker causing pain
Instead, it continued with utter disdain

But what of players and of the team
Should penalties given forever deem

Their accomplishments stolen without thought
I think not, their victories were hard-fought

Strike from history the wins and losses
But only from head coach and bosses

There is such a better way
To set an example and say

To victims whose childhood was cheated
By caretakers benched, forever defeated

To always remember
The game in September

Is not at all immune
So lives again not ruined

But let's all decide
Light be our guide

The future is today
So they will be okay

Pathfinder

Do we have to be hit on the head
Or go to sleep and dream in bed

To find our way, pursue life's dream
What to do impossible it may seem

Listen closely to universal clues
Trying to help find your just due

Happiness forever mere wish or promised state
Get aboard the train, it's never too late

Follow your course led by a pathfinder
What's that, you ask, a wish to be kinder

Or maybe a prayer to open up eyes
Seeing what's real removing ego lies

And before you know it, the world will change
Improving all lives and physical exchange

Change

What in the world is for me to do
This my friend is only up to you

Whether potential is met or lost
The world either wins or pays a steep cost

It's never too late to reach your calling
Whether your stature is rising or falling

It's simply a matter of wanting more
Then look inside to soul's inner core

The gift from the Source of all creation
Is only limited by our own imagination

Abraham was one hundred when starting a nation
So now is the time to request pure elation

Change
Rearrange

Go find
In your mind

A gift to be kind
Then thoughts rewind

And soon you will be
Forever happy, set free

Sandy

Historic storm winds of change
A hundred lives lost, a family estranged

Not giving in nor sharing any Light
Just some noise a senseless fight

Stay indoors, and hide from the pain
Releasing emotion tears fall like rain

Inner peace from introspection
Showing unconditional affection

What will your birthright be
Loving or hurricane Sandy

Trial, Smile

When confronted with a difficult task
Take in the Light remember to bask

What seems a problem you will face
Is an opportunity negativity erase

There is nothing you can't overcome
So welcome the challenge let in some

Don't run away be shy or hide
True blessings will be our guide

When feeling bothered is nearby
The darkness is just a 1 percent lie

Face the enemy, it is always within
Your certainty is how you will win

Your trial
Just smile

To show
Inner glow

Others gain
From refrain

Removing pain
Acting sane

Lend a Hand

When someone reaches out to you
Look at it through their eye view

What do they now truly need
No agenda in the giving deed

Simply share without a thought
A lesson not so easily taught

Do not seek or want acclaim
Share not even saying your name

The gift given comes right on back
Now realizing what the others lack

Is merely a reflection inside of you
Let others provide the sharing cue

And what is it that you receive
God Light, giving you wouldn't believe

Do not refuse
Universal clues

One day soon
No lives ruined

Be not righteous
In giving Light much

Rise Above

When you think you have it made
The empty feeling inside, visit paid

Lacking less seeming so unsure
You can accomplish so much more

Uncertainty must be done away
Your ego talking so silently say

I am not what I appear
I will do away with fear

There is more that I can be
Things I'm not my soul can see

Today I will rise high above
Yesterday a memory I shove

Each day
In play

Now sure
I do more

Rewire Your Brain

We walk this earth, bodies covered by skin
Not knowing who we are or where to begin

We act unthinking in material terms
A lifetime ending covered by worms

But that is just the 1 percent lie
Get selfish in finding out why

Our texture cannot be seen or felt
Essence of God ephemeral not held

Infinite in giving ability
Cut off by ego hostility

Close your eyes, imagine a place
Looking down from outer space

Or better yet pick a personal venue
That fits together like a favorite menu

Rewire your brain, smell the scent
Soulful permanence is heaven-sent

Forever lasting
Feast not fasting

Energy you be
So no hostility

Teach, Not Preach

There are people on this earth
Saying words to state our worth

Tapping into the Essence of all
Knocking down a darkened wall

When you meet one you will know
Listening to their clear word flow

Wisdom of what is given I beseech
Share the message teach not preach

Living knowledge that is newly planted
Not unleashing, shoutouts loudly ranted

Uncaring conversion is not what is sought
Modeling wisdom that was lovingly brought

Learn
To overturn

The ego
Amigo

And when you do
Start again anew

Real life change
Improves exchange

Reminder
Be kinder

Choices

One year ago came like yesterday
Not knowing what to do or say

Tapping into never-ending Light
Words flow from 99 percent height

Message delivered I know my path
Lessons to give so I do the math

The world, a place to take or share
How will you do and ultimately fare

Remind yourself as memories fade
A choice that by each is daily made

Words for friends
Is the gift I send

What's in a Name

Magic resides inside of these
Not merely meant to please

Existing from a time before
Creation of what's in store

Looking upon them have no doubt
Lessons of what we're all about

Seventy-two ways for you to learn
What's in a name, bright Light no burn

Certainty that you can be great
Overcome obstacles you create

Do More

Today done, I go to bed, a restless sleep
Trying not to dwell or let thoughts creep

About the past opportunity missed
No, tomorrow I will check off my list

The challenges that come before
Lovingly gifted so I can do more

Not meant to harm or hurt
Rather it's a universal flirt

A way of winking I know you
A gift given each day anew

What will you do when so presented
A bouquet that's so beautifully scented

Meaningful Lesson

What is the core of life's pursuit
Meaningful lesson at Source root

Sharing not done so you feel great
But when you do you cannot wait

To try again and you will find
Each of us when being kind

Connects to Light that was sole made
Even hidden its brightness won't fade

Unconditional giving forever meant
A message received that was soul sent

To remind us each and every one
A game never lost but always won

Unlimited

Never getting too high or low
It's a feeling inside you know

Giving or receiving so you rehearse
No sharing or caring drive-in reverse

Turn it around requires only this
Open up eyes, or you'll surely miss

Recognition each of us has a place
Unique in creation stares in our face

Time to reveal so don't hold back
Who you are not what you lack

Unlimited
Spirited

Creative Force

What is it that you have made
Walking in the deep end wade

No safety net you fly alone
Read directions no dial tone

Creative force comes over you
Connected to Source like a few

What is it that burns inside
A feeling that you cannot hide

Reflection that you reveal
Essence of truth others feel

What you unveil
Deliver and sail

What you create
Is special, great

Spread the Word

Communicate a message true
Don't hold back expand the view

Sent in person or by mail
A world united cannot fail

Illusion of the inner self
Ego stealing hidden wealth

Sharing words, always known
Not given to one so others loan

Knowledge that will transform each
Wisdom given from heaven's reach

Light up eyes that darkness veils
Spiritual teaching unlocking jails

Spread the Word
Once others heard

The world will change
All physical exchange

Rise Above Revisited

The secret that is life's great mystery
Existing before times written history

Perfect place of awesome Light
Given from the greatest height

Receiving all but nothing given back
Point of Light through smallest crack

A chance to be like the Creator
In this realm be so much greater

All together rise
Share truth, not lies

Open eyes
No surprise

We become
Love some

Distance

Staring up to midnight sky
Reaching out to touch so high

Try to reach the ray of Light
Knowing it is out of sight

Which is nearer, close to you
Heaven or one born next to

Perfection in the outer reach
Distance infinite so I beseech

Love unconditional, do as God
From highest mountain or lowly sod

Why we came to earth
Requested before birth

Every Day

A Valentine's Day to show our love
Fitting together like hand in glove

Selfish thoughts are done away
Focus on others at least for a day

The world becomes a better place
When we share our smiling face

So let's make a Valentine's pact
Removing 364 days we lack

Remember to share, our love to show
Every day then our Light will grow

By showing this daily action
Receive forever soul satisfaction

Transformation

Molded from a piece of clay
Where from, only one can say

Little more than a needy thing
Parental love my life you bring

Growing up an intelligent being
But higher form, I am not seeing

Conscious thoughts arrive from ego
Reactive response denying Light flow

Evolved in spirit deeds of giving
If desire is for more richly living

Transformation will one day come
Pick yourself up after falling some

Time Travel

What is this message received
Have I been forever deceived

Parallel in purpose stated in mind
A Universe searching ever will find

Infinite in mystery it seeks to reveal
Sands of an hour glass slipping I feel

Energy expands growing but not old
Time travel, a mystery each of us hold

Fear not the molecules that separate
Illusion of youth, return atom, create

Older age
Turn page

Dawn to eve
Time to leave

Or better yet stay
All-encompassing pray

Life's Journey

Set out on a course so you may do
Your life mission, spent to not rue

Each day given a chance to create
Better version of self, we don't hate

Perfection impossible, but strive for more
Allows truth expansion of no ceiling nor floor

Your soul's reality not a physical thing
What to the table will outer self bring

Physical realm, mere fiction, so fake
Give freely not worrying what to take

Space exists between each of us all
Our job to remove it, get up, if we fall

In so doing, we remember the one
Creative game that is never done

No one can ever here lose
Even unconscious taking a snooze

Whether or not earned
Listened to or learned

At the day's end
Back home send

In this lesson
No more guessing

Perception

Don't look to outer empty place
Blaming others show off face

The world is not happening to
Creation comes inside of you

God-given right from birth
When arrive on naked earth

A choice so clearly made
Manifesting dues repaid

And just when you really think
Mastering lessons now blink

Awakening from blissful sleep
Realizing knowledge is steep

Cannot ever be given back
Comes at a price, that's a fact

Share lesson then you see
Wisdom gained, always free

Never Be Afraid

It is a rare talent nay, a godlike gift
To share dreams with others, to uplift

Never be afraid to state your mind
In so doing, you will forever find

Your passion, your purpose, right before eyes
Sometimes masked or hidden behind ego lies

Peeling the onion requires only this
Conscious desire, then you never miss

Sharing your heart blesses you and more
Giving to others what they hope will restore

Faith that you can have everything desired
Doing so with love which never gets tired

Certainty breeds
Unlimited deeds

One day soon
Sixteen years in June

What does the future hold
Live life each day be bold

Princess Pudding

There is this girl like none who came before
A love Light shining through her very core

A beautiful spirit that breaths life's daily fun
Usually we see her then out the door she runs

Messy in her room okay sometimes, yes, it's true
If help is needed, she always will come through

Mischievous smile on that darling face
Want to hug her but off she goes to race

Growing tall I recognize her sweet heart
Even when letting out a really smelly fart

Yes, Princess Pudding, you're all of that and more
Can't wait for the next chapter to see what's in store

Bright eyes
Small size

Beautiful spirit
Without limits

The world is yours
find your cause

Mother's Day

What is there for me to say
Another year another day

Remembering mom for all you do
A family sharing each year anew

This message sent with all our love
Together fitted like a woolen glove

Snug and warm you make us feel
The love shown to each so real

Given free and without taking back
We love you so and that's a fact

One thing more I want to say
New bathrooms for all thanks to Na

Unending Certainty

Our short time together, it's hard to understand
In this world of illusion, to see a design so grand

Limitless in power when the soul is released
Our Essence is not body, but an energy beast

Unending in aspect, the real journey now begins
Releasing mortal issues, and false ideas of sins

Perfect in creation, there's no chance we can lose
Looking in on loved ones sharing in all their news

Knowing with certainty together in the end
Going home to Source whose Light God sends

Know in your heart
You're never apart

Energy Expansion
Limitless Mansion

Reactive State

Anger rage emotional burst
Mind unthinking, language cursed

Relations enraged, provides us a chance
Remove our reactive blind stubborn stance

Proactive thought wellness preserved
Giving each a life so richly deserved

Of hope and of Light of happiness felt deep
Removing all heartache, instilling love we reap

Here's the proactive formula:

1. Pause (don't react)
   Problem: The car is in front of you is going slowly or has cut you off. Identify your reaction: you need to get to an appointment and are impatient, it was personal so getting angry etc as you are being prevented from getting to your destination or being targeted. (If reacting in the moment occurs, try to remember next time it happens. There is a reason. Pause next time. Do not react.)
2. Instead, state "what a pleasure." (The acceptance/certainty that the moment was sent to you for a reason was not meant to hurt you. So now decide what the reason is.)
3. Not pleasure in an uncomfortable moment rather you knowing this opportunity is being sent by an intelligent Universe aware as a blessing to address something in your life (movie) so thank the Light, the Universe, for the opportunity to transform the lack and your typical reaction, giving you an opportunity to proactively pause

and transform (in this case to be more patient, to remove anger). If you miss the opportunity this time in your reaction, it's okay. Identify it afterward as an opportunity that you are getting closer. So next time, you'd proactively consciously pause.

4. Identify each opportunity sent, and act with proactive conscious restriction and thoughtful care (why this was sent and not label it as good or bad).

Asking creator universe light show me guide me help me (pray) sincerely.

Restriction giving up control on how to fix this. We don't have the strength; only the creator can take away the false fear, the worry, and the feeling of being lacking.

Friendly Fire

Tap into the never-ending Source
Then you become a creative force

Never-ending happiness lost is found
Unlimited potential is what abounds

Will you dare to ask the question
What is it well devise the best one

That takes you on your life's quest
Seeking truth have you yet guessed

Joy not found from outside another
Journey toward an inner brother

One day, the future is before
Did you open or leave shut doors

What is your soul when you set free
Not a mere body that's not reality

Erase illusion then you will find
Pursuit of what inside you divine

Death

Eyes closed
She reposed

Alive again
So I pen

End death
When body has left

Double Down

Twenty-one in blackjack can't be beat
A winning hand for all to greet

Twenty-one years we're together today
Twenty-one reasons for me to you say

A lucky man now stands before
Ready to double down for twenty-one more

And when it's over, the game all done
In each moment, our game will be won

Remember this
Our marital bliss

Started that day
When I met my Na

Future Now

Searching for your path in life
Look first inward prospects rife

Unlimited potential comes a price
Giving back much more than nice

Selfless act to nurture others
Pay a tithe to sisters and brothers

College-bound, you're ready now
Knowledge to gain and know how

Future now is where you are
Focus attention, and you'll go far

Entertainment major but more of this
Spiritual minor, and you'll learn bliss

Lifelong Song

While here what achieved
Given freely or just receive

A lifetime full of interaction
Positive or negative reaction

Today a new you make a choice
To continue same or now rejoice

Of all the people that you meet
How do you intend to each one greet

With a smile and love inside
Or hard shell which you reside

One day soon, it will be done
Toward funeral, or away run

Remembering a legacy of what
Greatness daily or life of not

Righteous Deeds

It's time to remember what is right
In order to do so, connect to the Light

Of the Creator who has an intended plan
Free will given, so passionate flames fan

What you desire is given with love
Emptiness only if selfishly put above

Give unconditionally do as God would do
Then you always gain your just due

Not because you wish to receive
Giving away freely a gift to relieve

Righteous deeds, not easily achieved
Removing ego feelings meant to deceive

In its place, a new feeling of satisfaction
Happiness always will be your life caption

Je Suis Charlie

It is not enough to decry the pain
Caused by those who are insane

Extremists come in all shapes and sizes
Vigilance against future attack surprises

Requires cooperation and outing those
Who hide in shadows to not be exposed

Like rats, they scatter when Light shines
Together we stand world, citizens define

"I am Charlie," our battle cry
He wasn't afraid of terror or to die

So if you know about a plot or a plan
Will you remain silent and quietly stand

Or choose to remove a global threat
Your reward being a hero's debt

Brave and true together we stand
Removing agony throughout our land

Conscious Testament

Conscious testament
What is the message sent

Where does the strength of rope derive
If not from strands of individual lives

Intertwining us all to supply a gift
Conscious spirit in Essence to lift

Testament to a spirit so unique and rare
When voices stand united to show we care

Not alone ever, but connected at seed core
To our French family, we say, je t'adore

You are not alone in our prayers we send
Through darkness together, our will shall not bend

Showing insanity there is a better way
To express our voices and get our say

Destruction of lives
Through cowardly lies

Leads to rebirth
World citizens of earth

Challenges

When facing your worst fear
Know the Light is close by near

Not allowing judgment in
Turning off your ego sin

Face the pain, and you will see
Expanding vessels are set free

Showing others a path to self
Revealing souls, absolute health

One day soon a world receives
A miracle forever to believe

Challenges seem
Difficult deemed

However instead
Lose the dread

And you will see
A world set free

(When we think we can't do anything about it, it's just easier not to think about it. A friend reminded me today that there is a growing field of scientific study surrounding healing called integrative medicine. It shows scientifically (look it up; there are many studies) the conscious power of healing in conjunction with traditional medicine. So I thought, let's all send our thoughts of healing to our friends in France today, and see if it helps. Here's my thought; you're welcome to use it or create your own. But together, we can each make a difference and help.)

Wake Up

A world alive with so many paths
Your job simply smile, have fun laugh

And not ignore the signs sent here
Peal the layers and remove the fear

No coincidence merely sent this
Challenges lift up not meant to dis

Respect for each and every one
Wake up, your call, don't walk, run

Changing each one lifting up
World ego given a sharing cup

Conscious change from I receipt
The lie revealed no more deceit

And soon we see a worldwide shift
Our Source has given, a forever gift

Physical plain
Remove disdain

A life to share
All over to care

Start again
Make a friend

And you will see
Never too late to be

Who you are
A shining star

Ban Terror Plan

What is there for us to say
When politics get in the way

Doing what's right is a tricky thing
When multiple layers of issues bring

Seeking accord of sanctions released
Not at the expense of nuclear war increase

Will we place in hands that seek
Destruction of all fanatical freaks

Limiting access to nuclear plans
Or put them in a zealot's hands

We have seen what havoc is wrought
To end the world war that countries fought

Nuclear devastation, there's no going back
Unless we change as a matter of fact

Ban
All terror fans

From nuclear access
Or face terror success

Mask Hides Truth

Walking around to unlock the key
When you look at what do you see

Hunger and famine create a divide
Homeless our family helps to provide

Mask hides a connection between
The current of life so easily seen

Release false fear, seek out the truth
Integration of unity a world we sooth

Masquerade of separation reality face
Reject war and instead an arms embrace

Interlock together united we march
Citizens nay, family, look over and watch

Looking out teach
Your hand outreach

Your face is mine
Connection a line

Back to our Source
Energy of course

When we let go
We stop the flow

50 Years of Memories

Growing up just down the block
A few years old so not a shock

Memories flood all over me
Taking out pictures from two or three

Your wedding day, a fairy tale
Fifty years together, time does sail

Buzz cut toy gun smuggled in
Carried out with a big old grin

Remembering you watched over me
Loaded diaper, my aunt and uncle flee

Now it's time, a new cousin born
Coming to visit each Sunday morn

Bungalow colony, Upstate New York
Together in Brooklyn, we get to talk

Moving away from down the block
Sad day for me, turn back the clock

Visiting together throughout the years
Crossing bridges, the sounds I hear

High school college entering the law
You remind me in life to daily explore

Kids growing up, to college and past
Marriage families our lives move fast

Watching each other never getting old
Rather creating memories, we get to hold

When I look at the two of you
I see pure love inside and through

So on this most special of days
Here is the toast I get to you say

My uncle and aunt whom I adore
You set ceilings with no limits or floors

Creating in others a feeling of hope
Facing daily challenges with tools to cope

Self-Portrait

When looking in your own mirror
What you and God sees may differ

Perfection of what do you strive
Reflection to live your own live

But at what cost if you should fail
At the end of life's journey tale

And should you to others compare
How if different gifts given is that fair

Mirror my reflection of self
I lift a glass to toast health

Happiness too is what we seek
An achievement somewhat bleak

But if you open your eyes and peak
The darkness and Light each do seek

To direct us and to help our lives reach
Our own best example and try to teach

Others
Our brothers
Sisters, mothers

To not point out blame
For our failure or fame

But rather in each moment decide
Who we are living or dying inside

Movie Time

Look deep inside what do you see
A frightened child so set me free

Mirror reflection of all that you are
Whether in your home or traveling far

No matter the place or who appears
It's a lesson to learn or to teach fears

But Light doesn't come from worry
It's false, it's fake, simply ego sonny

Wake up to reveal your inner truth
Remove pain like extracting a tooth

Change the channel its movie time
Shifting course simply shifts on a dime

Your life is yours to do as you choose
So what you decide is a win or a lose

Is always up to you what to do
Past a waste of time to rue

Simply do, now what
That's all you ever got

In a single second
Love or fear beckons

Prologue

If you enjoyed these writings from the first fifteen years of *soul songs*, let me share a few more. For a future without limits. Know you are loved, and you only need to ask to find your purpose.

As a scout, here is the next grouping. Where are you in your life? You can change your course or continue with one amazing thought. I am waiting to hear back.

Chapter 3
Love Pulls

A kite can fly up very far
By a cloud or near a star

Up, up, and away, flying it goes
Heading to a place only it knows

Wind guided surrounded by air
Seemingly floating without any care

But connected by hand to a string
With one gentle pullback, you bring

Love pulls like that letting us know
That wherever we may travel or go

An invisible string connects us tight
So never fear to take on a new flight

Coming back together, always so sweet
While away, there's new people to meet
Fly
High
Touch
Sky
Close
Eyes
See
Love's prize

Formula 4...

Emerson wrote of earthly success
With deep thought, of utter finesse

That the measure of it, not purely financial
Rather a feeling so much more substantial

Leaving our world a better place
He did it with a pen, letters not erase

By writing this formula in a way
A scout he, a message to display

What a gift this success to share
So others you be forever aware

Of the affection left with a child
Or a photo taken leaving smiles

It needn't be dollar contribution
Not wrong but an energy infusion

So when your legacy is left
Another will realize how blessed

That earth was lucky in your Presence
An individual who lived in such resonance

We each other can daily remind
To find joy inside so easy to find

Time in this reality
Requires a duality

Not merely to survive
Rather uplifting, others to thrive

(My *why* in life is to write words channeled by the Creator—reminders, messages of the infinite nature of potential, that anything is possible. However, each person's path in life is different; their connection to the Source is not the same. Once you learn your *why*, it's your choice whether and how to use it. For me, I require inspiration to tap into the Source for the word flow to come forth. My eldest son, reminded me of that. It can occur with resonant music, a sound, a picture, a person, or an idea, but feeling it is required.)

Money Blessed, Freedom Express

It's not about how much money made
All are blessed whether it's spent or saved

It's really all about the feelings inside
Follow emotion of joy, darkness deride

Time your way to express freedom yourself
Whether helping out others or taking on wealth

No judgment here by our Creator
All loving unconditional, not a hater

You choose to expand or remain static
No drama here unless you like it erratic

Mistakes are instructive; find what best fits
Activity or meditation, expansion or sit

In the end, the playground was created
To allow in physicality, experience satiated

It's not about the author—it's only about what the loving words mean to you...

So the reminders shared in *Soul Songs 1—the First 15 Years of Poetic Purpose* are now yours; use them as you will. For me, they continue to flow to the date of this writing.

Rather than presuming anyone will care to read any more of the journey, for those who do, you needn't wait.

Here is a compilation, a summary of "Life Rules," a Cliff Notes version of all given to the publication date. Use the list of reminders (emanations) that speak to you as you will and create (share) your own amazing path that sings to the world:

So if your body expired tomorrow, would you be afraid or... live knowing you are never-ending infinite energy and death is impossible?

You are not your body.

You are a son or daughter of God.

Mistakes are not mistakes they are simply experience that is expansive and can change.

That God doesn't ever judge, if you feel bad, change course.

If you like who you are, continue on that path.

Physicality is a safe playground with bumpers.

Live life in passion with abundance and joy.

22 Reminders (Emanations)

1. You chose to come here for a reason.
2. Things happen for you, not to you.
3. You are connected to the Source and are a cocreator of physical reality.
4. Learn your purpose/live your *why* (it's only a question and inner dialogue away).
5. Trust intuition (feelings); they're the best radar for your truth.
6. Find happiness and joy in the present moment.
7. Thoughts, words, and actions manifest matter.
8. Manifest faster when connected to joyful emotion.
9. Pain is instructive, not meant to harm; don't label it as good or bad.
10. The Source Creator is unconditionally loving always, no matter what you do. (If it feels wrong or dark, then simply change.)
11. Perfection is a fiction and limiting; live expansively.
12. Free will means you decide infinitely.
13. Be certain of your connection to the Creator; it is unbreakable and aware of you.
14. Physicality is a 1 percent reality—a safe playground—so dream big.
15. Your body is not who you are; it is merely a spacesuit. You are infinite energy.
16. Truth evolves and is expansive, not static.
17. The physical world was created for a reason.
18. Unconditional love is the answer to being like God.
19. Ego is the only true enemy.
20. Time is not linear; it's an all-encompassing moment.
21. Accept others on their path; we are each unique.
22. No one is above or below any other.

Things Happen for You, Not to You

The Universe is of you aware
Gifts given in each moment when shared

Never meant to hurt or foment
Creator, all-loving, no judgment sent

What is it you think should occur
With mind manifest, so it is served

How to make metaphysical form occurring
A thought is Light energy plus stirring

Then becomes matter with conviction
Emotional knowing, math formula, not fiction

Time not linear, a forever path pursuit
All-encompassing momentary route

Things happen for you, not to you
Reminder meant for a healthy living view

The rules of the game on this earth
Were made for each wizard at birth

Meaning the path soul navigates
Winding route with free will satiates

No mistakes here experience ever-expanding
So world by you made never is handing

In moments given, we each may create
Something inside felt so great

But if lesser than feeling your *why*
Ask yourself to pursue another try

When you do, please so state
With emotional connection satiate

Live in utter blissful joy
Path purpose these words do employ

About the Author

D. R. Scotte began his poetic path seeking life rules (channeled reminders) shortly after 9/11, trying to make sense of his bodily death being averted.

Twenty-two years ago, his wife handed him a book that set him on a metaphysical journey, resulting in his own inner conversations with God that generate loving, uplifting messages of hope.

For nearly two decades, he kept these messages to himself. However, her passing and friends' encouragement inspired him to share these teachings.

They are meant for anyone who wants to connect with our Creator and to be reminded that our unique journey is filled with purpose, with none above or below.

Printed in the USA
CPSIA information can be obtained
at www.ICGtesting.com
LVHW021239301124
797959LV00001B/166

* 9 7 9 8 8 9 1 3 0 5 0 8 3 *